KEY FIGURES OF THE VIETNAM WAR

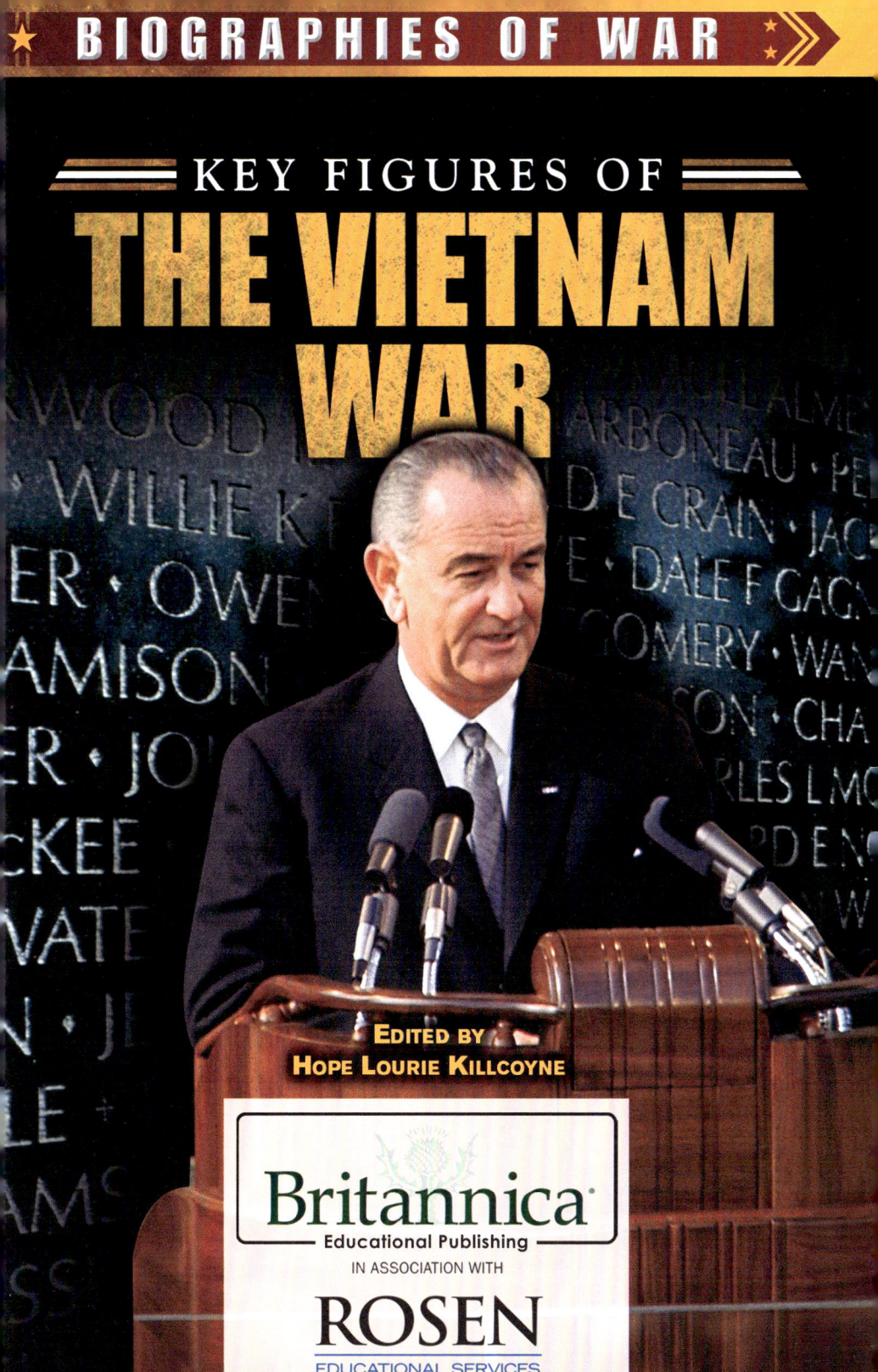

Published in 2016 by Britannica Educational Publishing (a trademark of Encyclopædia Britannica, Inc.) in association with The Rosen Publishing Group, Inc.
29 East 21st Street, New York, NY 10010

Copyright © 2016 by Encyclopædia Britannica, Inc. Britannica, Encyclopædia Britannica, and the Thistle logo are registered trademarks of Encyclopædia Britannica, Inc. All rights reserved.

Distributed exclusively by Rosen Publishing.
To see additional Britannica Educational Publishing titles, go to rosenpublishing.com.

First Edition

Britannica Educational Publishing
J.E. Luebering: Director, Core Reference Group
Anthony L. Green: Editor, Compton's by Britannica

Rosen Publishing
Hope Lourie Killcoyne: Executive Editor
Nelson Sá: Art Director
Michael Moy: Designer
Cindy Reiman: Photography Manager
Karen Huang: Photo Researcher
Introduction and additional text supplied by Hope Lourie Killcoyne.

Library of Congress Cataloging-in-Publication Data

Key figures of the Vietnam War/edited by Hope Lourie Killcoyne.— First edition.
   pages cm.—(Biographies of war)
Includes bibliographical references and index.
ISBN 978-1-68048-063-4 (library bound)
1. Vietnam War, 1961-1975—Biography—Juvenile literature. 2. Vietnam—Biography—Juvenile literature. 3. United States—Biography—Juvenile literature. I. Killcoyne, Hope Lourie, editor.
DS557.5.K49 2015
959.704'30922—dc23
                                                                                    2014044687

Manufactured in the United States of America

Photo credits: Cover and p. 3 (Johnson) Robert W. Kelley/The Life Picture Collection/Getty Images; cover and p. 3 (background) Dennis K. Johnson/Lonely Planet Images/Getty Images; pp. 6–7 (background) EastVillage Images/Shutterstock.com; p. 7 Howard Sochurek/The Life Picture Collection/Getty Images; p. 11 Sarawut Intarob/Moment/Getty Images; p. 13 Art Wolfe/Iconica/Getty Images; p. 15 www.jethuynh.com/Moment/Getty Images; pp. 16–17 © Digital Vision/Getty Images; pp. 18–19 Jack Cahill/Toronto Star/Getty Images; pp. 22–23 Kris Vandereycken/iStock/Thinkstock; p. 30 Archive Photos/Getty Images; pp. 32–33 Keystone/Hulton Archive/Getty Images; p. 35 National Archives and Records Administration; p. 37 Encyclopædia Britannica, Inc.; pp. 38–39 Paul Schutzer/The Life Picture Collection/Getty Images; pp. 40–41 Terry Fincher/Express/Archive Photos/Getty Images; p. 43 Universal Images Group/Getty Images; p. 44 Larry Burrows/The Life Picture Collection/Getty Images; pp. 46–47 Brian K. Grigsby, Department of Defense/The National Archives; pp. 48–49 © Everett Collection Inc/Alamy; pp. 54–55 Hugh Van Es/UPI/Landov; p. 60 Carlo Bavagnoli/The Life Picture Collection/Getty Images; pp. 64–65, 70–71, 72–73, 80-81, 94 © AP Images; p. 76 Mondadori/Getty Images; p. 83 PhotoQuest/Archive Photos/Getty Images; p. 87 Hulton Archive/Getty Images; pp. 90–91 Reuters/David Hume Kennerly/White House/Landov; pp. 92–93 AFP/Getty Images; p. 96 Focus On Sport/Getty Images; interior pages background textures Eky Studio/Shutterstock.com, Sfio Cracho/Shutterstock.com, Attitude/Shutterstock.com, macknimal/Shutterstock.com, Valentin Agapov/Shutterstock.com; back cover Oleg Zabielin/Shutterstock.com.

CONTENTS

INTRODUCTION 6

CHAPTER ONE
VIETNAM: THE COUNTRY, ITS
PEOPLE, AND THE ROAD TO WAR 10

CHAPTER TWO
THE STRUGGLE FOR INDEPENDENCE,
U.S. INVOLVEMENT, AND THE
SCARS OF WAR 29

CHAPTER THREE
ASIAN LEADERS 57

CHAPTER FOUR
AMERICAN LEADERS 78

CONCLUSION 99
GLOSSARY 101
FOR MORE INFORMATION 104
BIBLIOGRAPHY 107
INDEX 108

INTRODUCTION

The Asian country of Vietnam was wracked by war for much of the mid-20th century. After decades as a colony of France, Vietnam won its independence in 1954 and was then divided into two parts, North Vietnam and South Vietnam. North Vietnam set up a communist government. It wanted to unify the country under a single communist regime modeled after those of the Soviet Union and China. On the other side, the anticommunist government of South Vietnam wanted to keep Vietnam more closely aligned with the West. Soon, these competing interests led to war.

The conflict that pitted North Vietnam and its allies against South Vietnam and its allies—principally the United States—is called the Vietnam War. Tellingly, many Americans do not realize that in Vietnam the conflict is known as the American War. The two-decades-long conflict was more about an idea—communism versus anticommunism—than it was about a land grab or a wish to control natural resources. Looking at the big

INTRODUCTION | 7

Child commandos wait outside the Vietnamese army training headquarters, 1954.

picture, the Vietnam War was a manifestation of Cold War tensions between the communist Soviet Union and the anticommunist United States. North Vietnam received weapons and military advisers from the Soviet Union and China. The United States provided South Vietnam with advisers beginning in the 1950s and sent troops to fight in the war from 1965 to 1973. U.S. leaders believed that if Vietnam became a communist country, it would lead to the fall of neighboring states to the communists—an idea known as the domino theory.

In the end, the North was victorious, and Vietnam was reunited under communist rule. But more than 20 years of war—from 1954 to 1975—had devastated Vietnam. Entire villages and rice paddies had been destroyed. Vast areas of the countryside were left barren and unusable because of the effects of bombings, land mines, and the spraying of an herbicide called Agent Orange. Millions of Vietnamese had been left homeless. Not until 1995 did Vietnam release its official estimate of war dead: as many as 2 million civilians on both sides and some 1.1 million North Vietnamese soldiers and Viet Cong communist rebels. According to U.S. estimates, between 200,000 and 250,000 South Vietnamese soldiers died. More than 58,000 U.S. troops were killed or went missing as a result of the war. Their names are inscribed on the Vietnam Veterans Memorial in Washington, D.C. Among the countries that had smaller forces in

INTRODUCTION

Vietnam, South Korea suffered more than 4,000 dead, Australia more than 500, Thailand about 350, and New Zealand some three dozen.

Key Figures of the Vietnam War will not only profile those people who played instrumental roles in and leading up to this long and bitter conflict, it will also provide an overview of the country of Vietnam and a chronicle of the war itself.

CHAPTER ONE

VIETNAM: THE COUNTERY, ITS PEOPLE, AND THE ROAD TO WAR

One of the world's most populous countries, Vietnam occupies the easternmost part of mainland Southeast Asia. It has a long coastline, much of which fronts the South China Sea to the east and south. The country is bordered by the Gulf of Thailand to the southwest, Cambodia and Laos to the west, and China to the north. Its capital is Hanoi. As of 2013, the estimated population of this long, narrow country was nearly 90 million.

LAND AND CLIMATE

Mountains cover about two-thirds of the land, especially in the north. The major lowland areas are two deltas, which are plains that form around the mouth of a river. In the northeast the Red River forms a delta at the Gulf of Tonkin. The Mekong River forms an even larger delta in the south.

Farmers at work in 2013, harvesting in the rice terraces of Yen Bai, a small town in northern Vietnam

The climate of Vietnam is largely tropical, with warm to hot temperatures, plenty of rainfall, and high humidity. Differences in humidity, rainfall, and temperature are caused largely by changes in elevation. Vietnam's climate is dominated by monsoons—wind systems that change direction and bring rainfall seasonally. The north has a hot and humid wet season from about May through October. The remainder of the year is relatively warm and humid, with only light rains. A prolonged period of fog, cloudiness, and drizzle occurs from December through April in the central zone and coastal lowlands. The south is generally warmer than the north. Its temperatures vary little over the course of the year, but it has a distinct rainy season, from about June through November.

PLANTS AND ANIMALS

Forests of oak, beech, chestnut, pine, teak, and ebony trees cover about a third of the land. Bamboo plants grow in many places. Mangrove trees grow along the coast. Much of the central highlands is thickly forested. Huge areas of the country's forests have been cleared, however, by loggers and for agriculture and resettlement. During the Vietnam War the U.S. Army destroyed vast tracts of forest in the south. To combat deforestation, the government of Vietnam has begun programs to replant trees.

The forests are home to animals such as deer, elephants, tigers, leopards, bears, and monkeys.

Douc langurs (also known simply as doucs) are strikingly colored monkeys native to Vietnam, Laos, and Cambodia. They were pushed to the brink of extinction by years of war in the region as well as by intensive hunting.

Vietnam also has crocodiles, boars, jackals, otters, skunks, pythons, and flying squirrels.

PEOPLE AND CULTURE

Traditional Vietnamese culture reflects the strong influence of Chinese civilization. Nearly 100 years of French rule followed by American involvement instilled many Western cultural traits as well. The Vietnamese, however, continue to maintain their own culture through such customs as attaching great importance to the family and observing rites honoring their ancestors. The different cultures of Vietnam's numerous minority ethnic groups, on the other hand, generally show little Chinese influence, and many groups have adopted some Western traditions. Since the late 20th century, the rise of tourism in Vietnam and the relaxing of economic and political controls have increasingly exposed the country's people to international cultural influences.

ETHNICITY, LANGUAGE, AND RELIGION

Ethnic Vietnamese make up about 85 percent of the country's population. They live mainly in the lowlands, but 20th-century relocation programs also brought large numbers of them to the highlands. Vietnam's more than 50 different minority ethnic groups live primarily in the highlands. Among them are the Tay, Thai, Nung, Hmong, Khmer, and Cham.

VIETNAM: THE COUNTRY, ITS PEOPLE, AND THE ROAD TO WAR

Ethnic Chinese are another significant minority. Although large numbers of ethnic Chinese left Vietnam following reunification in the late 1970s, they remain one of the country's most populous minority groups and play an important role in business and trade.

Vietnamese, the language of the ethnic Vietnamese, is the country's official language. Some people speak English or Chinese as a second language. French, which was once widely spoken in Vietnam, has declined in use.

About half of the country's people are Buddhists. Most of them practice a distinctive form of Buddhism that developed in Vietnam over hundreds of years. About a tenth of the population practices a new

A young woman of the Cao Dai faith prays in a temple.

religion such as Cao Dai, a highly nationalistic combination of Confucianism, Daoism, Buddhism, and Roman Catholicism that appeared in the 1920s. About another tenth follows local, traditional religions involving numerous spirits, and less than a tenth is Christian, mainly Roman Catholic. Roman Catholicism was introduced into Vietnam in the 16th century and flourished especially under the French. Atheists and nonreligious people account for about a fifth of the population.

POPULATION AND SETTLEMENT PATTERNS

In the decade following reunification in 1975, Vietnam's population grew rapidly. The country worked to check this growth, however, and by the late 1980s the birth rate had begun to decline. Over the next 20 years the birth rate dropped from well above to notably below the world average.

VIETNAM: THE COUNTRY, ITS PEOPLE, AND THE ROAD TO WAR

Although increasing numbers of people have been moving from the countryside to urban areas since the late 20th century, more than two-thirds of

Hanoi has many historical and scenic places, including pagodas, a feature of many temples in Buddhism. Pagodas are usually erected as commemorative monuments.

BOAT PEOPLE

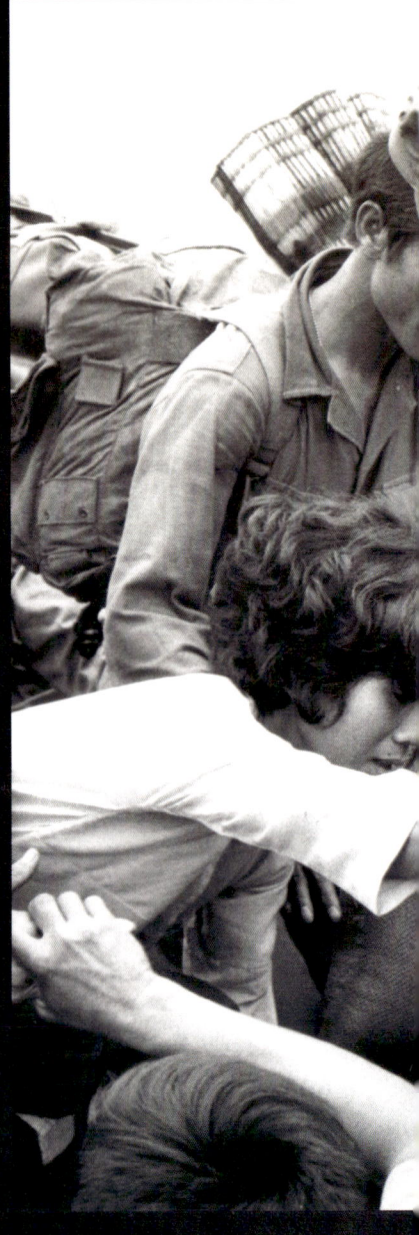

Emigration was substantial in the late 20th century. After the reunification of the country under communist rule, hundreds of thousands of people fled Vietnam, both legally and illegally, between 1975 and 1990. Relations with China were strained during this period. As a result of this situation and the transformation of the economic system in the south, the refugees included many ethnic Chinese, who were the target of discrimination. Many of Vietnam's refugees fled the country in small fishing vessels and thus became known as "boat people." An unknown number of them died at sea. Others entered refugee camps in Thailand and elsewhere or emigrated to other countries, especially the United States. In the 1990s large numbers of boat people were returned to Vietnam from the refugee camps. The last such camp closed in 2000.

VIETNAM: THE COUNTRY, ITS PEOPLE, AND THE ROAD TO WAR

Refugees flee Saigon, the capital of South Vietnam, in 1975.

the population lives in rural areas. The largest cities are Ho Chi Minh City and Hanoi.

EDUCATION AND HEALTH

The vast majority of Vietnam's people are literate. Education is universal and compulsory for five years of primary school and four years of lower-secondary school. Students can continue their education for three years of upper-secondary school in either an academic or vocational program. The government restructured the higher-education system in the 1990s and increased the number of universities and faculty members. Vietnam National University, with campuses in Hanoi and Ho Chi Minh City, is the country's largest university.

It was estimated that prior to the late 20th century only 15 percent of the population had access to safe water; more than 90 percent did in 2006. The government brought malaria largely under control and eliminated such major diseases as smallpox, polio, and leprosy. The prevalence of tuberculosis continued to be of concern, however, and the country experienced a major outbreak of avian influenza (bird flu) in the early 21st century.

ECONOMY

Vietnam is a developing country that has made significant strides in improving its economy. While the

VIETNAM: THE COUNTRY, ITS PEOPLE, AND THE ROAD TO WAR

country was divided in the mid-20th century, the two Vietnams had different economic systems. In communist North Vietnam the state planned the economy, owned and ran the industries, took control of the farmland, and organized farmers into cooperative units known as collectives. In South Vietnam many manufacturing industries were owned and run by the government, but private enterprise characterized other economic sectors, such as agriculture and trade. The people of the south enjoyed a significantly higher standard of living than those of the north.

Following reunification in 1976, the northern system was extended to the country as a whole. The government's efforts to abolish private property and to take control of industry, commerce, and farming in the south, however, met with resistance. The state-run economic programs were poorly run, and Vietnam suffered from an economic crisis.

In 1986 the government introduced a major reform program called *doi moi* ("renovation"), which began modernizing the economy and transforming the country into what it calls a "socialist-oriented market economy." In other words, like China, Vietnam has a socialist system that has embraced some elements of capitalism. Vietnam has moved away from having a centrally planned and subsidized economy. The government continues to own industries in many sectors and maintains overall control of the economy, but private enterprise is now tolerated in some sectors and the economy incorporates some market forces and incentives. Vietnam has also worked to

KEY FIGURES OF
THE VIETNAM WAR

reintegrate its economy with the global economy, opening the country to foreign investment and establishing trade relations with many more countries than before.

As a result of the country's economic reforms, the quality and variety of food, consumer goods, and exports improved and the volume of trade increased. The economy had previously been dominated by agriculture; manufacturing and service industries now grew in importance. Although the country's gross national income per capita was still low, it nearly quadrupled in the 20 years following the introduction of *doi moi*. Millions of people were lifted out of poverty.

AGRICULTURE

Agriculture—once the mainstay of the economy—still employs roughly half the labor force. Rice is the staple crop. The deltas of the Red and Mekong rivers, as well as other lowland areas, are

VIETNAM: THE COUNTRY, ITS PEOPLE, AND THE ROAD TO WAR | 23

Workers harvest rice in a paddy, or flooded field, in Vietnam.

the prime rice-growing regions. In many areas farmers grow two or three crops of rice per year, accomplished through an extensive system of irrigation. High-yielding varieties of rice are commonly used. Elsewhere such crops as cassava, corn (maize), sweet potatoes, sugarcane, coconuts, bananas, oranges, and pineapples are grown. Vietnam is one of the world's leading suppliers of cashews, black pepper, and rice. Among the other major cash crops are coffee, tea, peanuts (groundnuts), and rubber.

Before 1980 chronic food shortages caused widespread malnutrition. Natural disasters as well as collectivist policies were responsible for the food deficits. From the late 20th century, however, farms were run by individual families rather than by state collectives, and market-based incentives were used. Food production improved dramatically. While the country previously had to import food to feed its people, it began exporting large quantities of rice.

MANUFACTURING AND MINING

Manufacturing plays an important role in Vietnam, employing about one-seventh of the workforce. The largest industry is the processing of foods and beverages—especially seafood, coffee, and tea. The production of cement, fertilizer, and steel contributes greatly to the economy. Other major products include garments and cloth, shoes, electronics, tobacco products, transportation equipment, and paints, soaps, and pharmaceuticals.

Mineral resources, which are located mainly in the north, include coal, tin, chromium ore, and phosphates. The production of coal, crude petroleum, and natural gas are the most important mining activities. Vietnam's oil and gas deposits are located offshore in the South China Sea, mainly off the southern coast.

SERVICES

The importance of the service sector has grown significantly since the late 20th century. More than a quarter of the labor force works in service industries. Processing and assembly is a major component of this sector. Tourism, finance, marketing, scientific research, and telecommunications have become increasingly important.

Vietnam has greatly broadened its trade relations and liberalized its trade laws as part of its economic reform program. Prior to the late 1980s, the country's major trade partners were the Soviet Union and other communist countries. After the Soviet Union collapsed, Vietnam began trading more heavily with other Asian countries. After the Vietnam War, the United States imposed a trade embargo on Vietnam until 1994. The two countries ratified a major bilateral trade agreement in 2001, and the United States subsequently became the most important market for Vietnam's exports. Vietnam was granted membership in the World Trade Organization (WTO) in 2007.

TRANSPORTATION AND COMMUNICATIONS

The mountainous terrain of the central highlands limits land transportation between the north and the south to a narrow strip of land along the coast. Hanoi and Ho Chi Minh City are linked by rail and highway along this route. Two rail lines connect northern Vietnam to southern China. Vietnam has an extensive road network, though about half the roads are unpaved and many are in disrepair. In the two delta regions, vast networks of rivers and canals provide an important means of transport for smaller vessels. There are international airports serving Hanoi and Ho Chi Minh City. The state-owned carrier, Vietnam Airlines, offers both domestic and international flights.

The telecommunications system expanded dramatically after the economic reforms of the late 20th century. By the early 21st century, the number of main line telephones per capita was among the highest in Southeast Asia. The use of cell phones and the Internet has grown rapidly.

GOVERNMENT

Twenty-first-century Vietnam is a one-party socialist republic. The Vietnamese Communist Party is responsible for overall policy decisions and, according to the constitution, is the sole source of leadership for the government and society. The main government body

VIETNAM: THE COUNTRY, ITS PEOPLE, AND THE ROAD TO WAR

is the National Assembly, a one-house legislature that is directly elected by the country's citizens every five years. Most of the deputies have been members of the Vietnamese Communist Party, but some have been nonparty representatives. The National Assembly elects the president, who serves as head of state. The president nominates the prime minister, who is head of government and who leads a cabinet of ministers and other heads of government agencies. The judicial system includes courts at various levels, the highest of which is the Supreme People's Court.

HISTORY: FROM THE FIRST VIETNAMESE TO FRENCH RULE

In ancient times the ancestors of the Vietnamese lived in the north, in the Red River delta. In 207 BCE this area became part of the kingdom of Nam Viet, which included much of what is now southern China and the northern half of Vietnam. Nam Viet was conquered in 111 BCE by the Han Dynasty of China. The Chinese introduced their advanced civilization into the area and forced the Vietnamese to adopt Chinese customs and institutions. Chinese rule lasted for more than 1,000 years, until 939 CE, when the Vietnamese managed to throw off their conquerors. The Vietnamese kingdom expanded southward over the following 800 years, reaching as far as the Gulf of Thailand. Toward the end of this period, however, internal strife produced a struggle that lasted more than two centuries. Essentially, Vietnam was divided into two states, one in the north and one in the south. Following a civil war the country was reunited in 1802.

Political weakness permitted French intervention and expansion. France invaded Vietnam in 1858. In 1867 the south became a French colony known as Cochinchina, and in 1883 central and northern Vietnam became French protectorates known as Annam and Tonkin, respectively. Later all three were merged with Laos and Cambodia to form French Indochina. The French exploited the area as a source of raw materials for export, including rice, coal, and rubber. Throughout the period of French rule, strong nationalist and revolutionary movements began to grow as well.

CHAPTER TWO

THE STRUGGLE FOR INDEPENDENCE, U.S. INVOLVEMENT, AND THE SCARS OF WAR

At the start of World War II (1939–45)—nearly a century after France's first invasion of Vietnam—Vietnam and the rest of Indochina were still a French colony. During the war, however, Japan occupied Vietnam. In 1943 a Vietnamese nationalist group known as the Viet Minh began fighting the Japanese for Vietnam's freedom. The group was led by the communist revolutionary Ho Chi Minh—a man who was to play a major role in Vietnamese history. Ho's Viet Minh liberated much of northern Vietnam from Japanese control.

After Japan lost World War II, Ho declared Vietnam's independence on September 2, 1945. France, however, believed that Indochina was still rightfully its colony and was determined to retake control. By the end of the year, the French had seized southern Vietnam, but the Viet Minh

Ho Chi Minh

THE STRUGGLE FOR INDEPENDENCE, U.S. INVOLVEMENT, AND THE SCARS OF WAR

retained control of the north. From 1946 to 1954 the Viet Minh fought France in what became known as the First Indochina War. The United States, which was opposed to the spread of communism, helped fund and equip the French. Ho built support among the Vietnamese people and waged an increasingly successful guerrilla war from bases in the countryside. After suffering a major defeat in 1954, France decided to pull out of Vietnam.

DIVISION OF VIETNAM

The peace accords of 1954 officially ended French rule. They also temporarily divided the country at the 17th parallel of latitude in order to separate Ho's Viet Minh and the French forces. In the north was the Democratic Republic of Vietnam, or North Vietnam. It was led by Ho and had a communist government. Its capital was Hanoi. In the south a U.S.-backed, anticommunist government led by Ngo Dinh Diem took control. It became the Republic of Vietnam, or South Vietnam. Saigon (now Ho Chi Minh City) was its capital.

According to the peace accords, Vietnam was to be reunified in 1956, after elections for a new government were held. The North's Viet Minh leaders enjoyed wide popularity and seemed certain to win. For this reason, the United States and the government of South Vietnam never allowed the vote to take place, leaving the country divided.

GUERRILLA WAR IN THE SOUTH

Diem's rule of South Vietnam grew increasingly repressive. He used totalitarian methods to silence opposition, installed his family members in key positions of power, and failed to enact promised land reforms. He also gave preferential treatment to Roman Catholics, though most of the people were Buddhists. These actions embittered the Vietnamese and helped to bolster Ho's popularity.

A guerrilla force now known as the Viet Cong emerged in the South to oppose Diem's regime. By 1957 they had begun a program of terrorism, assassinating South Vietnamese government officials.

THE STRUGGLE FOR INDEPENDENCE, U.S. INVOLVEMENT, AND THE SCARS OF WAR

South Vietnamese president Ngo Dinh Diem at a fair near Saigon on March 7, 1957, shortly after an attempt on his life was foiled. He would be overthrown and killed in a military coup on November 2, 1963.

They ultimately killed tens of thousands of people associated with the government. The group was formed and led by communists, including many former members of the Viet Minh who lived in the South. They were soon joined, however, by numerous noncommunists who opposed the dictatorial regime. In 1959 the Viet Cong launched an armed insurgency to overthrow Diem and reunify Vietnam. The following year the National Liberation Front (NLF) was formed as the political arm of the Viet Cong. The Viet Cong were trained and armed by North Vietnam.

Despite its U.S. training, the army of South Vietnam was ill-prepared to combat the insurgency. It was not well adapted to fighting in the

TACTICS OF THE VIET CONG

For the most part, the Viet Cong fought a guerrilla war of ambush, terrorism, and sabotage. Frequently the Viet Cong attacked at night, withdrawing afterward to the security of the jungle. The Viet Cong's forces included full-time soldiers as well as villagers who lived at home and acted as part-time guerrillas. These villagers harassed the government, police, and security forces with booby traps, mines, raids, kidnappings, and murders.

THE STRUGGLE FOR INDEPENDENCE, U.S. INVOLVEMENT, AND THE SCARS OF WAR

A Viet Cong soldier crouches in a bunker in 1968, during the Vietnam War.

swamps and jungles. Many of its leaders were incompetent or corrupt. As the Viet Cong grew stronger, the U.S. government expanded its involvement in South Vietnam, starting in 1961 under President John F. Kennedy. Kennedy was assassinated in November 1963. By that time, about 16,000 U.S. troops had been sent to Vietnam as military advisers.

Popular opposition to Diem continued to grow. Buddhist monks and nuns held many demonstrations, and a few burned themselves to death in protest. Images of the Buddhists on fire were widely publicized and became a source of embarrassment to the United States. In November 1963, a few weeks before Kennedy was killed, Diem's army overthrew and assassinated him. The United States did not oppose the coup. Diem's replacement, however, was ineffective. South Vietnam's military seized control in 1965 and installed another oppressive regime under Nguyen Cao Ky and Nguyen Van Thieu.

Meanwhile, the Viet Cong insurgency seemed increasingly likely to succeed. Believing that victory was near, North Vietnam began sending army troops to fight in the South in April 1964. China and the Soviet Union decided to send military and economic aid to the North. U.S. military advisers had begun to assume a more active role in helping the South that included sabotage, espionage, and orchestrating Southern Vietnamese attacks on the North.

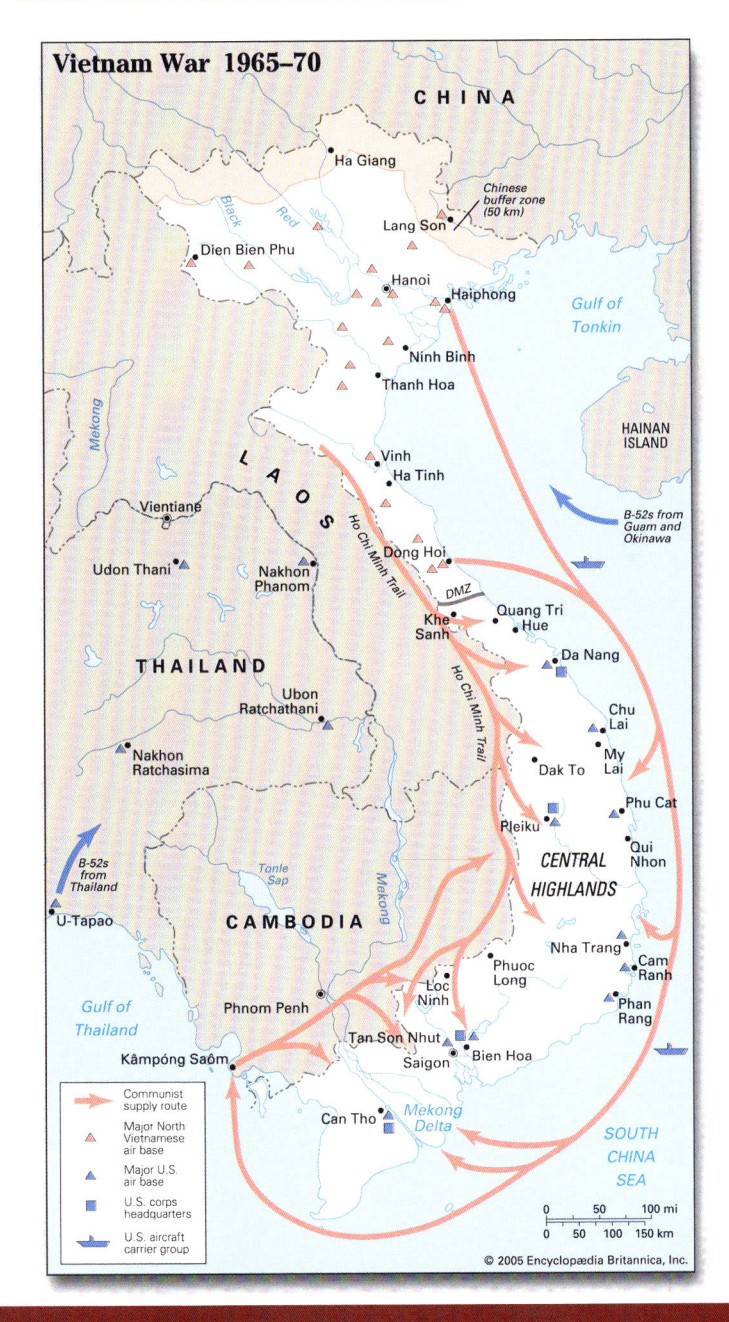

THE STRUGGLE FOR INDEPENDENCE, U.S. INVOLVEMENT, AND THE SCARS OF WAR

A map of North and South Vietnam during the Vietnam War shows major air bases and the communists' supply routes, including the Ho Chi Minh Trail.

GULF OF TONKIN RESOLUTION

On August 2, 1964, North Vietnamese torpedo boats attacked a U.S. ship, the destroyer USS *Maddox*. The destroyer was in the Gulf of Tonkin, off the coast of North Vietnam, on an intelligence mission. It suffered no damage from the attack. Two days later North Vietnamese torpedo boats allegedly attacked the *Maddox* and another U.S. destroyer. Although evidence for the attacks was inconclusive, U.S. President Lyndon B. Johnson ordered retaliatory air attacks against North Vietnamese naval bases. He also asked Congress to pass a broad resolution authorizing him to take whatever actions he deemed necessary to prevent or respond to future attacks on U.S. forces or allies in Southeast Asia. Congress quickly passed the measure, which became known as the Gulf of Tonkin Resolution. It allowed Johnson to send U.S. forces to fight in Vietnam without having to ask Congress to officially declare war.

THE U.S. ENTERS THE WAR

The Gulf of Tonkin incident strengthened American public support for military intervention in Vietnam. Johnson and his advisers took advantage of this support to adopt new, aggressive strategies. In February 1965, after a Viet Cong attack on U.S.

With weapons lifted above the water, U.S. Marines wade through a marsh in Vietnam, 1965.

troops at Pleiku, Johnson ordered the first in a series of sustained bombings of North Vietnam. The bombings, called Operation Rolling Thunder, were initially intended to end the traffic of North Vietnamese soldiers and weapons along the Ho Chi Minh Trail. The missions were later expanded throughout the North. Large numbers of civilians were killed by the strikes, which included the use of cluster bombs and napalm. The North fought the U.S. bombers with the aid of radar, antiaircraft guns, missiles, and jet fighters supplied by the Soviets and Chinese. By the end of the war the United States had dropped nearly 7 million tons of bombs on Vietnam. The bombing seemed to have little impact, however, on the ability of North Vietnam and the Viet Cong to carry on the war.

General William Westmoreland was the U.S. Army commander in Vietnam. After the launch of the bombing campaign in the North, he asked Johnson to send U.S. troops to fight a ground war in the South. Johnson did send ground forces, but without a declaration of war. The first troops landed in Da Nang in March 1965. By 1968 the number of U.S. troops in Vietnam had surpassed 500,000. Fighting alongside them were about 600,000 South Vietnamese

THE STRUGGLE FOR INDEPENDENCE, U.S. INVOLVEMENT, AND THE SCARS OF WAR | 41

troops, about 50,000 South Korean troops, and smaller contingents from Thailand, Australia, the Philippines, and New Zealand.

The U.S. forces had enormous and superior firepower. Westmoreland employed his troops in the jungles and mountains where the strongest enemy units were based. His goal was not to capture and

A group of U.S. Marines, armed with grenades, near the Laos border, 1968. The number of African American soldiers who participated in the war was disproportionately high.

MY LAI MASSACRE

One of the most notorious search-and-destroy missions carried out by U.S. soldiers during the Vietnam War took place in the village of My Lai on March 16, 1968. In that incident—known as the My Lai Massacre—as many as 500 unarmed civilians were killed.

My Lai was located in an area believed to be a stronghold of the Viet Cong and thus a focus of the U.S. military. After receiving word that Viet Cong were in the village, a company of U.S. soldiers was sent there on a search-and-destroy mission. Although no armed Viet Cong were found, the soldiers nonetheless killed all the women, elderly men, and children they could find; few villagers survived. The incident was initially covered up by high-ranking army officers, but it was later made public by former soldiers. In the ensuing courts-martial, platoon leader Lieutenant William Calley was accused of directing the killings, and in 1971 he was convicted of premeditated murder and sentenced to life in prison; five other soldiers were tried and acquitted. Many, however, believed that Calley had been made a scapegoat, and in 1974 he was paroled. The massacre and other atrocities revealed during the trial divided the U.S. public and contributed to growing disillusionment with the war.

THE STRUGGLE FOR INDEPENDENCE, U.S. INVOLVEMENT, AND THE SCARS OF WAR

Vietnamese villagers photographed during the My Lai Massacre, March 16, 1968

KEY FIGURES OF
THE VIETNAM WAR

occupy territory. Instead, he sought to fight a "war of attrition," inflicting such enormous losses on the communists that they would no longer be able or willing to fight. One way the United States tracked its progress in the war was the "body count"—a tally of the number of Viet Cong and North Vietnamese soldiers killed. These estimates, however, were widely viewed as inaccurate.

A major tactic was the "search-and-destroy" mission, in which U.S. forces would patrol for

U.S. Army soldiers burn down Vietnamese huts, 1968.

THE STRUGGLE FOR INDEPENDENCE, U.S. INVOLVEMENT, AND THE SCARS OF WAR

North Vietnamese and Viet Cong units and then obliterate their bases and personnel. The part-time guerrillas wore no uniforms, however, and they blended in with the civilian population. U.S. troops burned entire villages and captured or killed villagers suspected of collaborating with the communists.

A guerrilla war, the struggle in Vietnam was never concentrated along a single front. Most of the battles were small and brief, involving fewer than 200 fighters and lasting a few hours or less. Although the communists suffered heavy casualties, the guerrillas could always retreat to sanctuaries in nearby Cambodia, Laos, and North Vietnam. They also established a large network of underground tunnels. When U.S. forces withdrew, the guerrillas would return. The dense forests hid the guerrillas' movements as well as their supply lines and bases. To eliminate the forest cover, the U.S. Air Force sprayed millions of gallons of an herbicide called Agent Orange over large areas of South Vietnam. Agent Orange was also sprayed to kill crops that might supply the communists with food. Although the herbicide effectively killed vegetation, it caused major ecological damage. It also destroyed the civilians' food crops. In addition, the use of Agent Orange exposed thousands of Vietnamese and U.S., Australian, and New Zealand servicemen to potentially toxic chemicals. This exposure later caused serious health problems.

AGENT ORANGE

The herbicide Agent Orange, a toxic mixture of chemical substances used to destroy or stop plant growth, was used by U.S. military forces in Vietnam from 1962 to 1971. Among the Vietnamese, exposure to Agent Orange is considered to be the cause of an abnormally high incidence of miscarriages, skin diseases, cancers, birth defects, and congenital malformations (often extreme and grotesque) dating from the 1970s. Many U.S., Australian, and New Zealand servicemen who suffered long exposure to Agent Orange in Vietnam later developed a number of cancers and other health disorders.

THE STRUGGLE FOR INDEPENDENCE, U.S. INVOLVEMENT, AND THE SCARS OF WAR

A U.S. helicopter sprays defoliant over a jungle during the Vietnam War, 1969.

U.S. ANTIWAR MOVEMENT

Americans were deeply divided about the war. The movement that developed to protest the Vietnam War was the largest and most influential in U.S. history. Some Americans were opposed to the war from early on. Many of them objected to the war on moral grounds, often because of the large number of civilian casualties. They also wanted their government to stop supporting South Vietnam's repressive dictatorship.

As U.S. casualties began to mount and with no end to the war in sight, more Americans began to oppose the country's involvement. Many began to think that the war was unwinnable and too costly. By the end of 1967 nearly 500 U.S. servicemen were dying every week. At the time, more than half of all Americans were dissatisfied with the war.

Antiwar demonstrations first became common on college campuses. By 1967 a wide variety of protests were being held all over the country. The movement ultimately attracted Americans from all parts of society, but especially students, liberal Democrats, intellectuals, religious leaders, civil rights activists, pacifists, women's groups, prominent artists and musicians,

THE STRUGGLE FOR INDEPENDENCE, U.S. INVOLVEMENT, AND THE SCARS OF WAR

and later many politicians. Thousands of returned Vietnam veterans also opposed the war.

The vast majority of the antiwar protests were nonviolent. They included mass demonstrations, peace vigils, letter-writing campaigns, political organizing, acts of civil disobedience, and campus educational meetings known as "teach-ins." Protests occasionally turned or were designed to be

This iconic photo of the U.S. antiwar movement shows a young man placing flowers into the barrels of soldiers' rifles, 1967.

violent—a few, for example, involved the bombing of government buildings. Antiwar demonstrations sometimes provoked violent reactions from the authorities—notably at the 1968 Democratic National Convention in Chicago and at Kent State University in Ohio in 1970. At Kent State, the National Guard fired into a crowd of protesters, killing four students.

Protests also involved resistance to the draft. The U.S. forces fighting the war included large numbers of men who had been drafted, or called up for compulsory military service. Over the course of the long conflict, more than 1.8 million men were drafted. As the war progressed, increasing numbers of men burned their draft registration cards in protest. Some activists raided and otherwise tried to disrupt the draft boards. In addition, about a half million people evaded, or "dodged," the draft. Many of them, famously including heavyweight boxer Muhammad Ali, simply refused to report for service when called. Other draft dodgers fled the country, in many cases to Canada.

Journalism played an important role in shaping American opinion about the war. Opposition to the war was strengthened, for example, by newspaper excerpts of the top-secret defense department reports known as the Pentagon Papers in 1971. These articles exposed lies told by the U.S. government to the American people concerning its intentions in Vietnam.

The Vietnam War was the first conflict to be extensively televised, and the coverage was daily and graphic. Images and reports from the battlefield often seemed to call into question the official U.S. position on how well the war was progressing. Much of what the public could see of the war on television appeared confusing if not futile—notably during the 1968 Viet Cong and North Vietnamese attacks known as the Tet Offensive.

THE TET OFFENSIVE

In early 1968 the Viet Cong and North Vietnamese forces launched a large-scale offensive throughout the South. It occurred during Tet, a Vietnamese holiday celebrating the lunar new year, while an informal cease-fire was in place. Some 84,000 communist troops simultaneously attacked more than 100 cities and military bases on January 31, including the U.S. embassy and General Westmoreland's headquarters in Saigon. Before the offensive, the communists had mounted a number of diversionary attacks to attract U.S. forces away from the big cities. When the Tet Offensive began, some 50,000 U.S. troops were thus already busy defending bases in other areas.

The Tet Offensive ended in a military victory for the U.S. and South Vietnamese forces. Although taken by surprise, they recaptured all the bases and cities except Hue within a few days. The offensive turned out to be a major psychological victory for the communists, however. The U.S. government had been claiming that victory was near. The American public was shocked to see that, on the contrary, the North showed no signs of weakening or losing resolve. Many began to believe that the United States was locked in a stalemate.

PEACE TALKS OPEN, FIGHTING CONTINUES

After the Tet Offensive, President Johnson was faced with increased antiwar sentiment and political pressure to pull out of the conflict. In March 1968 he ordered an end to the bombing of North Vietnam, except near the border with the South. Peace talks between the United States and North Vietnam began in May but were quickly deadlocked. The ground war intensified, leading to the conflict's fiercest fighting. In November the United States halted the bombing over the entire North. South Vietnam and the Viet Cong joined the peace talks in January 1969.

Meanwhile, a new U.S. president, Richard M. Nixon, had been elected. Henry Kissinger was one of Nixon's chief foreign policy advisers. Nixon and Kissinger recognized that the United States could not win the war. They insisted, however, on an "honorable" peace settlement that would give South Vietnam a reasonable chance for survival. A hasty withdrawal, they contended, would damage U.S. credibility internationally.

Nixon began to gradually withdraw U.S. ground troops in 1969. Through a program called Vietnamization, the United States began transferring control of the ground war to the South

THE STRUGGLE FOR INDEPENDENCE, U.S. INVOLVEMENT, AND THE SCARS OF WAR

Vietnamese forces. The troop withdrawals were popular among the American public. To many U.S. soldiers still in Vietnam, however, the withdrawals seemed to emphasize the apparent pointlessness of the war. Morale among the troops was already low. Major problems included drug abuse, desertion, and even violence against officers.

Although Nixon reduced the number of U.S. soldiers in Vietnam, he resumed the bombing of North Vietnam. He also expanded the war into Cambodia and Laos. Nixon ordered secret bombing missions of the communists' sanctuaries and supply lines in Cambodia in 1969–70 and in Laos in 1970. He also authorized an incursion across the Cambodian border by a U.S. and South Vietnamese force of 20,000 men. News of this invasion increased American public opposition to the war. Meanwhile, the peace talks continued to stagnate.

In 1972 the North mounted a large invasion of the South. In response, the United States bombed North Vietnam as well as the invasion forces in the South. U.S. forces also mined the harbor at Haiphong, where the North received Soviet supplies. The North's invasion soon failed.

THE END OF THE WAR

After this defeat, the leaders of North Vietnam signaled that they were ready to compromise in the peace talks. Kissinger and Le Duc Tho of North Vietnam secretly began to negotiate a peace treaty. Later in the year, however, a setback in the talks led Nixon to order an intensive 11-day bombing mission of Hanoi and other northern cities.

Finally, on January 27, 1973, a peace treaty was signed by the United States, South Vietnam, North Vietnam, and the Viet Cong. A cease-fire began the following day. According to the treaty, the South Vietnamese were to have the right to determine their own future. North Vietnamese soldiers who were already in the South were allowed to remain there but could receive no reinforcements. An international force was established to keep the peace.

U.S. troops left Vietnam by the end of March 1973. Fighting continued, however, as the North and the South accused each other of truce violations. The fighting was less intense, though, than it had been before the cease-fire. The United States began cutting military and economic aid to the South.

THE STRUGGLE FOR INDEPENDENCE, U.S. INVOLVEMENT, AND THE SCARS OF WAR

The ultimate fall of South Vietnam began with the North's capture of Phuoc Long Province in January 1975. In March the North Vietnamese launched

Another iconic image from the war era, this photo captures the desperation of the fall of Saigon as dozens of South Vietnamese are evacuated via a helicopter perched atop a small building on April 29, 1975. This helicopter was one of the last to take evacuees from Saigon to U.S. Navy ships waiting off the coast of Vietnam.

a major invasion to capture the South, which they expected to take two years. Within two months, however, additional inland provinces and several coastal cities had fallen, with little resistance from Southern troops.

South Vietnam surrendered on April 30, 1975, as Northern troops entered Saigon. A military government was set up in the South until Vietnam was officially reunited on July 2, 1976. The country became the Socialist Republic of Vietnam, with its capital at Hanoi. Saigon was renamed Ho Chi Minh City.

CHAPTER THREE

ASIAN LEADERS

Military, political, and ideological leaders from Vietnam and the neighboring region ranged from Ho Chi Minh, the president of North Vietnam who fought to make Vietnam a united, independent, and communist country, to the devout Catholic and fervently anticommunist president of South Vietnam, Ngo Dinh Diem.

KEY FIGURES FOR NORTH VIETNAM

When the war began in 1954 and the country was split into two parts, many Vietnamese leaders (from the North *and* the South but on the side of the North) wanted to reunite the country under communism. Eventually, their dream came true.

HO CHI MINH
(1890–1969)

As founder of the Indochinese Communist Party in 1930 and president of North Vietnam from

1945 to 1969, Ho Chi Minh led the longest and most costly 20th-century war against colonialism. His whole adult life was devoted to ending French and, later, American domination of Vietnam. His goals were achieved in 1975, six years after his death, when the last Americans left South Vietnam.

Ho was born Nguyen Tat Thanh on May 19, 1890, in Hoang Tru, Vietnam (then known in the West as French Indochina). He attended school in Hue during his teen years, worked as a schoolmaster for a time, and went to a technical school in Saigon. In 1911 he went to work on ocean freighters, which took him around Africa and as far as Boston and New York City. After two years in London (1915–17) he moved to Paris and remained there until 1923. While in Paris he became a socialist and organized a group of Vietnamese living there in a protest against French colonial policy.

Inspired by the successful communist revolution in Russia, he went to Moscow in 1924 and took part in the fifth Congress of the Communist International. His anticolonial views kept him from returning to Vietnam until the end of World War II. Much of his time was spent in China, where he organized the Indochinese Communist Party on February 3, 1930. It was in about 1940 that he began to use the name Ho Chi Minh, meaning "he who enlightens."

In 1941 Ho and his comrades formed the League for the Independence of Vietnam, or Viet Minh. By 1945 the Japanese had overrun Vietnam and defeated the French, and later in the year the Japanese were defeated by the United States. Ho immediately sought the cooperation of the United States in preventing the return of colonial rule, and on September 2, 1945, he proclaimed the independence of Vietnam.

This proclamation was premature: two Indochina wars were fought before Vietnam became independent. Ho's main contribution during the wars was keeping both the Soviet Union and China from gaining too great an influence in Vietnam. Although his death was reported on September 3, 1969, in Hanoi, the Vietnamese Communist Party disclosed in 1989 that Ho had actually died on September 2, Vietnam's National Day.

LE DUC THO
(1911–1990)

During the Vietnam War, Le Duc Tho directed the Viet Cong guerrilla force in its insurgency against the South Vietnamese government. He later played a pivotal role in cease-fire negotiations with the United States, which supported South Vietnam during much of the war.

Originally named Phan Dinh Khai, Le Duc Tho was born on October 14, 1911, in Nam Ha province, Vietnam. From an early age, he was active in political movements aimed at securing Vietnamese independence from France, which then controlled much of the Indochinese peninsula, including Vietnam. With Ho Chi Minh, he became one of the founders of the Indochinese Communist Party in 1930. He spent much of the

Le Duc Tho poses in front of a portrait of Ho Chi Minh during one of the Paris Peace Conferences, June 11, 1969.

ASIAN LEADERS   61

1930s and early '40s as a prisoner of the French authorities. From 1945 Tho helped lead the Viet Minh, a communist-oriented group seeking independence from France and the ouster of Japanese forces that occupied Vietnam during World War II. After the Japanese surrendered to the Allies in September 1945, the Viet Minh seized the capital, Hanoi, proclaiming Vietnam's independence. War with France ensued, lasting until 1954, at which time Tho was named to the Politburo, or leadership council, of the Vietnam Workers' Party, which later became the Vietnamese Communist Party.

With the country divided at the end of the war into communist North Vietnam and anticommunist, U.S.-backed South Vietnam, Tho assumed oversight of the Viet Cong, the South Vietnamese guerrilla force that, with the support of the North Vietnamese army, fought for reunification against South Vietnam and the United States. He carried out most of his duties during the Vietnam War while in hiding in South Vietnam.

Tho is best known for his part in the Paris Peace Conferences, which met from 1968 to 1973 to negotiate a cease-fire in Vietnam. He eventually became the North Vietnamese delegation's chief spokesman, in which capacity he negotiated the cease-fire agreement that led to the withdrawal of the last American troops from South Vietnam. For this accomplishment he was coawarded the Nobel Peace Prize with Henry Kissinger of the United States. Tho declined to accept the honor, declaring that peace had not yet been established in Vietnam.

Not surprisingly, the peace agreement between the two Vietnams soon broke down, and in 1975, Tho played a leading role in the full-scale North Vietnamese invasion that finally overthrew the South Vietnamese government and brought the two countries together under communist rule. In 1978 he played a similar role in the first stages of Vietnam's invasion of neighboring Cambodia. Tho remained an influential member of the Politburo until 1986, though he never became its leader. He died in Hanoi on October 13, 1990, one day before his 79th birthday.

VO NGUYEN GIAP
(1912–2013)

Vietnamese general Vo Nguyen Giap was renowned for helping to liberate his country from French colonial rule.

Giap was born in 1912 in An Xa, Vietnam. The son of an anticolonialist scholar, as a youth he began to work for Vietnamese autonomy. He attended the same high school as Ho Chi Minh, and while still a student in 1926 he joined the Tan Viet Cach Menh Dang, the Revolutionary Party of Young Vietnam. In 1930, as a supporter of student strikes, he was arrested by the French and sentenced to three years in prison, but he was paroled after serving only a few months. After studying at the Lycée Albert-Sarraut in Hanoi, he received a law degree from Hanoi University in the late 1930s. Giap then became a professor of history at the Lycée Thanh Long in Hanoi, where he converted many of his fellow teachers and students to his political views. In 1938 he married Minh Thai, and together they worked for the Indochinese Communist Party. When in 1939 the party was prohibited, Giap escaped to China, but his wife and sister-in-law were captured by the French police. His sister-in-law was guillotined; his wife received a life sentence and died in prison after three years.

In 1941 Giap formed an alliance with Chu Van Tan, guerrilla leader of the Tho, a minority tribal group of northeastern Vietnam. Giap hoped to build an army that would drive out the French and support the goals of the Viet Minh, Ho Chi Minh's Vietnamese independence movement. With Ho Chi Minh, Giap marched his forces into Hanoi in August 1945, and in September Ho announced the independence of Vietnam, with Giap in command of all police and internal security forces and commander in chief of the armed forces. Giap sanctioned the execution of many noncommunist nationalists, and he censored nationalist newspapers to conform with Communist Party directives. In the French Indochina War, Giap's brilliance as a military strategist and tactician led to his winning the decisive battle at Dien Bien Phu on May 7, 1954, which brought the French colonialist regime to an end.

On the division of the country in July, Giap became deputy prime minister, minister of defense, and commander in chief of the armed forces of North Vietnam. He subsequently led the military forces of the North to eventual victory in the Vietnam War, compelling the Americans to leave the country in 1973 and bringing about the fall of South Vietnam in 1975. From 1976, when the two Vietnams were reunited, to 1980 Giap served as Vietnam's minister of national defense; he also became a deputy prime minister in 1976. He was a full member of the Politburo of the Vietnamese Communist Party until 1982. Giap was the author of *People's War, People's Army* (1961). He died in Hanoi on October 4, 2013.

NORODOM SIHANOUK
(1922–2012)

Cambodian leader Norodom Sihanouk served as king of Cambodia, prime minister, exiled leader, president, and king again. He proved to be a resilient leader of a country torn apart by civil war.

Born in Phnom Penh, Cambodia, on October 31, 1922, Sihanouk was educated at French schools in Vietnam, China, and France. In April 1941, during World War II, he became monarch for the first time. Cambodia was still a French protectorate at the time. The Nazi-backed Vichy government in Paris thought he would be a more easily manipulated ruler than his father. After

ASIAN LEADERS | 65

Prince Norodom Sihanouk and his wife, Monineath, in Phnom Penh, Cambodia, November 1969

the war he negotiated for Cambodia's sovereignty, and France granted the country independence in 1953. In 1955 Sihanouk abdicated in favor of his father and formed the People's Socialist Community, which won national elections that year. He became the new king's foreign minister and prime minister. In 1960, after the death of his father, Sihanouk accepted the role of head of state.

Sihanouk proclaimed a policy of neutrality in his foreign policy. Nevertheless, during the Vietnam War he allowed Vietnamese communists to operate covertly from bases inside eastern Cambodia in return for a North Vietnamese pledge to respect Cambodia's frontiers. He subsequently rejected U.S. aid and assistance, relying on his immense popularity with the Cambodian people to keep radicals of both the right and the left under control. Under Sihanouk's rule, Cambodia experienced 15 years of fragile peace and mild prosperity while much of Southeast Asia was in a state of upheaval.

In 1970, while on a foreign tour, Sihanouk was overthrown. He then created a government-in-exile in Beijing and made allies of North Vietnam and the rebel Cambodian Khmer Rouge army. In 1975, when the communist government of Cambodian dictator Pol Pot assumed power, Sihanouk returned as head of state. He resigned in 1976 and was under house arrest until 1979, when he went into exile in China.

During the next decade Sihanouk helped direct the struggle against Cambodia's Vietnamese-installed government and embraced the Khmer Rouge. In 1991 the four main factions vying for power in Cambodia agreed to establish a Supreme National Council that would rule the country under the chairmanship of Sihanouk before elections could be held in 1993. The elections resulted in a coalition government with Sihanouk's son Prince Ranariddh as first prime minister and Hun Sen as second prime minister. The new constitution restored the monarchy and made Sihanouk king for the second time. Hun Sen overthrew Prince Ranariddh in 1997, but he left Sihanouk on the throne. Sihanouk abdicated in 2004 and was succeeded by his son Norodom Sihamoni. Sihanouk died on October 15, 2012, in Beijing, China.

KEY FIGURES FOR SOUTH VIETNAM

During the war years South Vietnam had a number of political leaders, the longest regimes being those of Ngo Dinh Diem and Nguyen Van Thieu. None of these leaders, however, was successful in preventing the communist takeover of the country.

NGO DINH DIEM
(1901–1963)

Vietnamese leader Ngo Dinh Diem was a strong nationalist and anticommunist. He served as president, with dictatorial powers, of South Vietnam from 1955 until his assassination in 1963.

Diem was born on January 3, 1901, in Hue in northern Vietnam. He belonged to one of Vietnam's noble families, and in his youth he was on friendly terms with the Vietnamese imperial family. His ancestors in the 17th century had been among the first Vietnamese converts to Roman Catholicism. In 1945 Diem was captured by the forces of the communist leader Ho Chi Minh, who invited him to join his independent government in northern Vietnam. But Diem rejected the proposal and went into self-imposed exile, living abroad for most of the next decade.

In 1954 Diem returned at the emperor Bao Dai's request to serve as prime minister of a U.S.-backed government in South Vietnam. After defeating Bao Dai in a government-controlled referendum in October 1955, he ousted the emperor and made himself president of the newly declared Republic of Vietnam (South Vietnam). Diem refused to carry out the Geneva Accords, which had called for free elections to be held throughout Vietnam in 1956 in order to establish a national government.

With the South torn by dissident groups and political factions, Diem established an autocracy that was staffed at the highest levels by members of his own family. With U.S. military and economic aid, he was able to resettle hundreds of thousands of refugees from North Vietnam in the South, but his own Catholicism and the preference he showed for fellow Roman Catholics made him unacceptable to Buddhists, who were an overwhelming majority in South Vietnam. Diem never fulfilled his promise of land reforms, and during his rule communist influence grew among southerners as the communist-inspired Viet Cong launched a guerrilla war against his government. The military tactics Diem used against the insurgency were heavy-handed and ineffective and served only to deepen his government's unpopularity and isolation.

Diem's imprisoning and killing of hundreds of Buddhists, who he alleged were abetting communist insurgents, finally persuaded the United States to withdraw its support from him. Diem's generals assassinated him during a coup on November 2, 1963.

LON NOL
(1913–1985)

Lon Nol was a Cambodian soldier and politician. His 1970 overthrow of Prince Norodom Sihanouk involved Cambodia in the Vietnam War and ended in the 1975 takeover of the country by the communist Khmer Rouge.

Lon Nol was born on November 13, 1913, in Prey Vêng, Cambodia. He entered the French colonial service in 1937. He joined the army in 1952 and fought against intruding Vietnamese communist guerrillas in Cambodia as an area commander. In 1955 he became Cambodian army chief of staff, and in 1960 he was named commander in chief. He was deputy premier (1963), minister of defense (1968–69), and twice premier (1966–67

KEY FIGURES OF
THE VIETNAM WAR

A uniformed Lon Nol saluting, March 29, 1975. Three days later he left Cambodia for the United States, where he remained for the rest of his life.

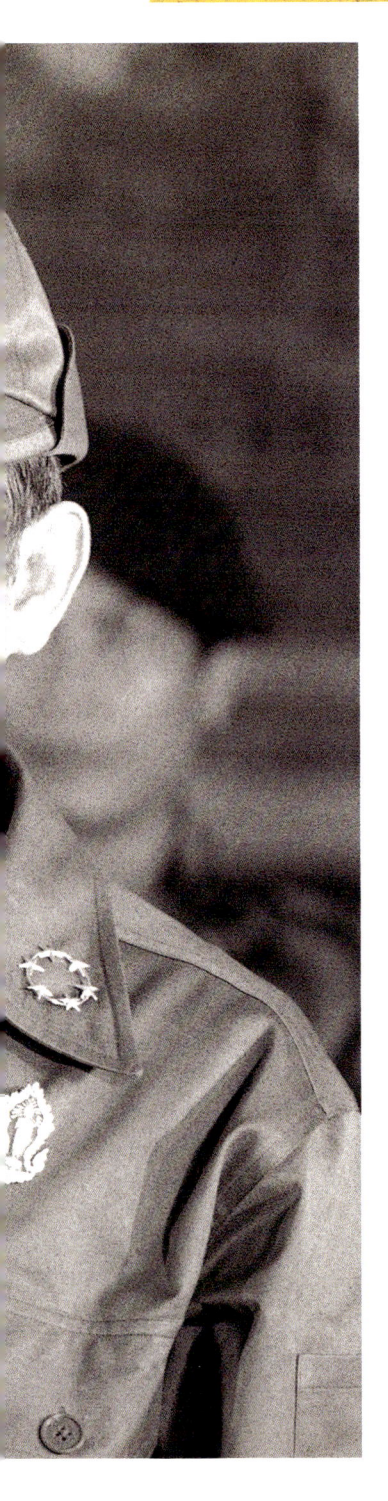

and from 1969) under the country's leader, Prince Norodom Sihanouk.

Lon Nol was a prime architect of the coup in March 1970 that overthrew Sihanouk, and he became the most prominent leader in the new government, serving as its premier until 1972. Abandoning Sihanouk's policy of neutrality in the Vietnam War, Lon Nol established close ties with the United States and South Vietnam, permitting their forces to operate on Cambodian territory. He assumed total power over Cambodia on March 10, 1972, and installed himself as president two days later. In the meantime, the communist Khmer Rouge movement was gathering strength in the Cambodian countryside, despite a U.S. air campaign against the insurgents. On April 1, 1975, with Khmer Rouge guerrillas only a few miles from the capital, Lon Nol left the country and settled in the United States. He died in Fullerton, California, on November 17, 1985.

KEY FIGURES OF THE VIETNAM WAR

NGUYEN VAN THIEU
(1923–2001)

Nguyen Van Thieu was president of South Vietnam from 1967 until it fell to the forces of North Vietnam in 1975.

The son of a small landowner, Thieu was born on April 5, 1923, in Ninh Thuan province, a coastal region in southern Vietnam. He joined the Viet Minh in 1945 but later fought for the French colonial regime against the Viet Minh. In 1954 he was put in charge of the Vietnamese National Military Academy, and, after 1956, he continued to serve under the regime of Ngo Dinh Diem in South Vietnam. Thieu played an important part in a successful coup against Diem in 1963. In 1965 he became chief of state in a military government headed by Premier Nguyen Cao Ky. In 1967 he was elected president under a new constitution put in place in that year. He was reelected without opposition in 1971.

Thieu's emergence coincided with the beginning of major U.S. intervention in the Vietnam War. Despite criticism of the authoritarian nature of his regime, he retained the support of the United States throughout the administrations of the U.S.

ASIAN LEADERS | 73

presidents Lyndon B. Johnson and Richard M. Nixon. He continued to consolidate his power after the peace agreements of 1973 and the withdrawal of U.S. troops from South Vietnam.

Communist gains in South Vietnam's northern provinces early in 1975 prompted Thieu to recall

South Vietnamese President Nguyen Van Thieu and U.S. President Richard M. Nixon at a press conference in San Clemente, Califiornia, April 2, 1973

troops to defend the capital city, Saigon (now Ho Chi Minh City). Badly managed, the retreat was not just chaotic but also a devastating defeat, allowing communist forces to surround the capital. After resisting for several days, Thieu was persuaded that his resignation might permit a negotiated settlement of the war. On April 21, 1975, in a speech denouncing the United States, he resigned in favor of his vice president, and shortly afterward he left the country. He went first to Taiwan and later to England before settling in the United States. He died in Boston, Massachusetts, on September 29, 2001.

NGUYEN KHANH
(1927–2013)

Nguyen Khanh was a military and political leader who participated in a successful coup against the South Vietnamese dictator Ngo Dinh Diem in 1963. He served briefly as president of South Vietnam in 1964.

Khanh was born on November 8, 1927, in Tra Vinh, in southern Vietnam. He served in the French colonial army until 1954 and rose through the ranks of the Vietnamese army to become chief of staff to General Duong Van Minh. He joined Minh and other high military officials in assassinating Diem on November 1, 1963, and led a counter-coup against Minh in 1964. Khanh served variously as president or prime minister of South Vietnam in January–October 1964; he briefly held both posts.

His regime was undermined by several coups, and he himself resigned once. After four junior officers took control of the government in February 1965, Khanh was named roving ambassador but was, in effect, exiled to the United States. He settled in California, where he later served as the head of a government-in-exile. He died in San Jose, California, on January 11, 2013.

NGUYEN CAO KY
(1931–2011)

Nguyen Cao Ky led South Vietnam as prime minister for two years (1965–67) during the Vietnam War. He was known for his flamboyant manner and militant policies.

Ky was born in Son Tay, in northern Vietnam, on September 8, 1930. He joined the South Vietnamese Air Force after the nation was partitioned in 1954. He attracted much attention because of his vehement anticommunism as well as his bravado, and he was highly favored by U.S. advisers in Vietnam. As a result he was named commander of South Vietnam's air force after the 1963 overthrow of the Ngo Dinh Diem government. With U.S. aid, Ky soon built up a fighting force of 10,000 men.

In June 1965 Ky, together with Major General Nguyen Van Thieu and South Vietnamese General Duong Van Minh, led a military coup in unseating the government of Premier Phan Huy Quat.

Nguyen Cao Ky during a parade in Saigon, 1968

As the head of that trio, Ky provoked widespread opposition to his authoritarian policies. In 1967 the top military leaders reached an agreement by which Thieu would run for president and Ky for vice president of a new regime. Unhappy with his new position, Ky became an outspoken critic of Thieu's administration. In 1971 he attempted to oppose Thieu for the presidency but was forced to remove himself as a candidate and returned to the air force. Upon the fall of South Vietnam in April 1975, Ky fled to the United States. He died on July 23, 2011, in Kuala Lumpur, Malaysia.

CHAPTER FOUR

AMERICAN LEADERS

The United States provided economic and military aid to South Vietnam from the beginning of the Vietnam War. It entered the war directly in 1965 by bombing North Vietnam and sending its first ground troops. By 1968 the United States had more than 500,000 troops in Vietnam. Key American figures range from political and military leaders to those people who led the antiwar movement.

POLITICAL AND MILITARY FIGURES

LYNDON B. JOHNSON: HIS ROLE IN THE VIETNAM WAR
(1908–1973)

Lyndon Baines Johnson, also called LBJ, was the 36th president of the United States

(1963–69). A moderate Democrat and vigorous leader in the United States Senate, Johnson was elected vice president in 1960 and became president in 1963 upon the assassination of President John F. Kennedy. During his administration he signed into law the Civil Rights Act (1964), the most comprehensive civil rights legislation since the Reconstruction era, initiated major social service programs, and bore the brunt of national opposition to his vast expansion of American involvement in the Vietnam War.

Johnson was born on August 27, 1908, on a farm near Stonewall, Texas, the eldest of five children. He was elected to the U.S. House and Representatives in 1937 and to the Senate in 1948. He made his way to the White House as vice president for John F. Kennedy. The assassination of President Kennedy on November 22, 1963, plunged Johnson into the country's highest office.

As president, Johnson faced grave problems in the nation's foreign affairs, particularly in Southeast Asia. After North Vietnam attacked U.S. destroyers in the Gulf of Tonkin in August 1964, he ordered U.S. armed forces to conduct retaliatory attacks. The role of the United States in the Vietnam War escalated in 1965. In March U.S. planes began bombing military targets in North Vietnam. In June American forces in South Vietnam joined in the fighting. Throughout the year, numerous proposals for discussions to end the conflict were made directly by Johnson or through private diplomatic talks; all were rejected by North Vietnam. In a major peace-seeking effort, Johnson suspended bombing raids late in 1965 and sent personal representatives on peace missions to capitals throughout the world. North Vietnam's rejection of these efforts led to the resumption of bombing on January 31, 1966.

As the United States expanded its participation in the war, bipartisan criticism of Johnson's policies grew. Johnson dwelt heavily on the Vietnam problem in his 1967 State of the Union message. From then onward, antiwar sentiment gradually spread among many segments of the population, including liberal Democrats, intellectuals, and civil rights leaders. As his popularity sank to new lows, Johnson was confronted by demonstrations almost everywhere he went. It pained him to hear protesters, especially students—whom he thought would venerate him for his progressive social agenda—chanting, "Hey, hey, LBJ, how many kids did you kill today?" To avoid the demonstrations, he eventually restricted his travels, becoming a virtual prisoner in the White House.

AMERICAN LEADERS | 81

On March 31, 1968, under the pressure of domestic problems and increasing antiwar sentiment, the president announced a curtailment of bombing in North Vietnam and once again proposed peace talks to the North Vietnamese. He renounced his candidacy for a second term

In March 1968, with protests against the Vietnam War growing, U.S. President Lyndon B. Johnson announced that he would de-escalate the war and would not seek reelection that year.

in order to free his hand for peace negotiations. Peace talks began in Paris in May but quickly became stalemated. Johnson broke the impasse by ordering a total cessation of the bombing of North Vietnam, effective November 1.

Johnson was succeeded by Richard M. Nixon, a Republican, on January 20, 1969. On January 22, 1973, Johnson suffered a fatal heart attack at his Texas ranch, just a few days before the end of the fighting in Vietnam.

WILLIAM WESTMORELAND
(1914–2005)

William Westmoreland was the U.S. Army officer who commanded American forces in the Vietnam War from 1964 to 1968.

He was born on March 26, 1914, in Spartanburg County, South Carolina, After his education at the Citadel and the United States Military Academy at West Point, he served with the 9th Infantry Division throughout World War II. In June 1964 Westmoreland became commander of U.S. forces in Vietnam, a post he would hold for the next four years.

Westmoreland decided on a war of attrition, one in which the enemy body count was the key measure of merit and "search and destroy" was the dominant tactical approach. In response to repeated requests from Westmoreland for more forces, the American commitment eventually grew

William Westmoreland at his desk in Vietnam, 1966

to well over a half million troops. Despite inflicting very heavy casualties on communist forces, that approach faltered as the enemy was more than able to make up the losses.

After the Tet Offensive of January 1968, Westmoreland faced a number of challenges, both in Vietnam and at home. The surprise attacks by North Vietnamese and Viet Cong forces in South Vietnam on dozens of towns, cities, airfields, and military bases, including Westmoreland's headquarters and the U.S. embassy in Saigon, shocked the American public. Although the offensive was an unqualified failure from a strictly military standpoint, news and images of the attacks completely undermined the assurances by Johnson and Westmoreland that the war was being won. In the wake of the attacks, Westmoreland was sent home to become army chief of staff; he retired in 1972. Westmoreland died on July 18, 2005, in Charleston, South Carolina, and was buried at West Point.

ROBERT S. MCNAMARA
(1916–2009)

Robert S. McNamara served as the U.S. secretary of defense from 1961 to 1968. He revamped Pentagon operations and played a major role in the country's involvement in the Vietnam War.

Robert Strange McNamara was born on June 9, 1916, in San Francisco, California. He earned a graduate degree at the Harvard Business School and later worked his way up to the presidency of the Ford Motor Company. After just one month as Ford's president, however, McNamara resigned to join the Kennedy administration as secretary of defense.

McNamara initially supported the deepening military involvement of the United States in Vietnam. On visits to South Vietnam in 1962, 1964, and 1966, the secretary publicly expressed optimism that the National Liberation Front (the political arm of the Viet Cong) and its North Vietnamese allies would soon abandon their attempt to overthrow the U.S.-backed Saigon regime. He became the government's chief spokesman for the day-to-day operations of the war and acted as President Lyndon B. Johnson's principal deputy in the war's prosecution.

As early as 1965, however, McNamara had privately begun to question the wisdom of U.S. military role in Vietnam, and by 1967 he was openly seeking a way to launch peace negotiations. He initiated a top-secret full-scale investigation of the American commitment to Vietnam, came out in opposition to continued bombing of North Vietnam, and in February 1968 left the Pentagon.

In 1995 McNamara published a memoir, *In Retrospect: The Tragedy and Lessons of Vietnam*, in which he describes the anticommunist political climate of the era, mistaken assumptions of foreign policy, and misjudgments on the part of the military that combined to create the Vietnam debacle. In Errol Morris's 2003 documentary film *The Fog of War*, McNamara discusses his career in the Pentagon as well as U.S. failures in Vietnam. He died on July 6, 2009, in Washington, D.C.

RICHARD NIXON: HIS ROLE IN THE VIETNAM WAR
(1913–1994)

Richard Nixon was the 37th president of the United States (1969–74). Faced with almost certain impeachment for his role in the Watergate scandal, he became the first American president to resign from office. He was also vice president (1953–61) under President Dwight D. Eisenhower, the 34th president of the United States.

Richard Milhous Nixon was born in Yorba Linda, a farming village in Orange County, California, on January 9, 1913. In August 1942 he joined the U.S. Navy, serving in World War II as an aviation ground officer in the Pacific and rising to the rank of lieutenant commander. Following his return to civilian life in 1946, he was elected to the U.S. House of Representatives. Four years later he was elected to the Senate. From 1953 to 1961 he served as vice president under President Dwight D. Eisenhower.

Nixon won the presidency in 1968 after campaigning on a platform promising "peace with honor" in Vietnam. After taking office, he gradually reduced the number of U.S. military personnel there. Under his policy of "Vietnamization," combat roles were transferred to South Vietnamese troops, who nevertheless remained heavily dependent on American supplies and air support. At the same time, however, Nixon resumed the bombing of North Vietnam (which had been suspended by President Johnson in October 1968) and expanded the air and ground war to neighboring Cambodia and Laos. In the spring of 1970, U.S. and South Vietnamese forces attacked North Vietnamese sanctuaries in Cambodia, which prompted widespread protests in the United States.

U.S. President Richard Nixon, during a nationwide television broadcast in 1970, directs viewers' attention to a map of Southeast Asia.

After intensive negotiations between national security adviser Henry Kissinger and North Vietnamese foreign minister Le Duc Tho, the two sides reached an agreement in October 1972, and Kissinger announced, "Peace is at hand." But the South Vietnamese raised objections, and the agreement quickly broke down. A new agreement was finally reached in January 1973 and signed in Paris. It included an immediate cease-fire, the withdrawal of all American military personnel, the release of all prisoners of war, and an international force to keep the peace.

The predominant issue of Nixon's second term was the unfolding of the political scandal known as Watergate, which eventually led to his resignation in 1974. Vice President Gerald Ford succeeded him on August 9, 1974. Nixon died on April 22, 1994, in New York City.

HENRY A. KISSINGER
(born 1923)

The most influential foreign policy figure in the administrations of U.S. presidents Richard Nixon and Gerald Ford was Henry Kissinger. He was the most notable exponent of shuttle diplomacy, making frequent trips overseas to solve complex international problems.

Henry Alfred Kissinger was born in Fürth, Germany, on May 27, 1923. He came with his parents to the United States in 1938 to escape the Nazi persecution of Jews. After receiving his doctorate at Harvard University in 1954, he taught there and became professor of government in 1962. His great expertise in matters of national security and strategic planning led to his appointment as national security adviser by President Nixon in 1969. He was secretary of state from 1973 to 1977.

Although he originally advocated a hard-line policy in Vietnam and helped engineer the U.S. bombing of Cambodia in 1969–70, Kissinger later played a major role in Nixon's Vietnamization policy—the disengagement of U.S. troops from South Vietnam and their replacement by South Vietnamese forces. On January 23, 1973, after months of negotiations with the North Vietnamese government in Paris, he initialed a cease-fire agreement that both provided for the withdrawal of U.S. troops and outlined the machinery for a permanent peace settlement between the two Vietnams. For his Vietnam negotiations he shared the Nobel Peace Prize in 1973 with Le Duc Tho of North Vietnam. He received the Presidential Medal of Freedom in 1977.

GERALD FORD: HIS ROLE IN THE VIETNAM WAR
(1913–2006)

Gerald Ford became the 38th president of the United States when his predecessor, Richard Nixon, resigned over the Watergate scandal. He was in office when the Vietnam War finally came to an end.

Gerald Rudolph Ford was born on July 14, 1913, in Omaha, Nebraska. As a high-school student, he waited on tables and washed dishes at a restaurant to earn money. Having been a football star in both high school and college, as a college graduate he refused offers from the Green Bay Packers and the Detroit Lions to play professional football. Ford earned a law degree from Yale University, served in the U.S. Navy in World War II, and eventually entered the political arena.

Ford was elected to Congress in 1948 and served for 25 years. During his time in Congress, he developed a reputation for honesty

AMERICAN LEADERS 91

U.S. Secretary of State Henry Kissinger updates President Gerald Ford on the situation in South Vietnam at the White House, April 29, 1975.

ANTIWAR VOICES

Benjamin Spock

American pediatrician Benjamin Spock was the most influential child-care authority of the 20th century. He was also known for his involvement in the peace movement.

Benjamin McLane Spock was born on May 2, 1903, in New Haven, Connecticut. He attended Yale University's medical school and received his medical degree from Columbia University in 1929.

From its first appearance in 1946, Spock's *Common Sense Book of Baby and Child Care* served as the definitive child-rearing manual for millions of American parents in the "baby boom" that followed World War II. Spock's approach was criticized as overly permissive by a minority of physicians, and he was even blamed for having helped form the generation of young Americans that protested the Vietnam War and launched the youth counterculture movement of the 1960s.

Spock's bitter opposition to U.S. involvement in the Vietnam War during the 1960s led to his trial and conviction in 1968 for counseling draft evasion—a conviction overturned on appeal. In 1972 he was the presidential candidate of the pacifist People's Party. Spock died on March 15, 1998, in La Jolla, California.

AMERICAN LEADERS 93

Linking arms with the Reverend Martin Luther King, Jr., Benjamin Spock participates in a demonstration against the Vietnam War in New York City, 1967.

KEY FIGURES OF THE VIETNAM WAR

Jane Fonda

Jane Fonda is an American movie actress and the daughter of actor Henry Fonda. She is also known for her political activism.

Born on December 21, 1937, in New York City, Fonda established herself as an actress with roles in socially conscious films in the 1960s and '70s. In the '70s and '80s she became active on behalf of left-wing political causes. An outspoken opponent of the Vietnam War, Fonda journeyed to Hanoi in 1972 to denounce the U.S. bombing campaigns there. During that trip she visited with the crew of a North Vietnamese air defense battery, and photographs of Fonda

Jane Fonda, standing in front of a "Defeat Nixon" poster with the Nazi swastika used in place of the X, addresses the crowd at an antiwar rally in San Francisco, August 24, 1972.

in the seat of an antiaircraft gun were widely circulated. Her actions led to her being branded "Hanoi Jane." In 1988 she apologized to American veterans of the Vietnam War in a televised interview with journalist Barbara Walters, saying that some of her behavior in Hanoi was "thoughtless and careless."

Muhammad Ali

One of the greatest American heavyweight boxing champions, Muhammad Ali was known as much for his flamboyant self-promotion and controversial political stances as for his boxing ability. He became the first boxer to win the heavyweight title three times.

Ali was born Cassius Marcellus Clay in Louisville, Kentucky, on January 17, 1942. He began boxing as an amateur at the age of 12. As a professional fighter, he gained immediate fame when he defeated heavily favored Sonny Liston on February 25, 1964, to win the world heavyweight title. After the Liston bout, Clay announced that he had joined the Nation of Islam, and he soon took the name Muhammad Ali.

Ali dominated the heavyweight division for the next three years. Then, on April 28, 1967, citing his religious beliefs, Ali refused induction into the U.S. Army at the height of the Vietnam War. This refusal followed a blunt statement voiced by Ali 14 months earlier: "I ain't got no quarrel with them Vietcong." Many Americans strongly condemned Ali's stand. It came at a

KEY FIGURES OF
THE VIETNAM WAR

Boxer and social activist Muhammad Ali is interviewed by sports commentator Howard Cosell after a heavyweight fight in the mid-1970s.

time when most people in the United States still supported the war in Southeast Asia. Although exemptions from military service on religious grounds were available to qualifying conscientious objectors who were opposed to war in any form, Ali was not eligible for such an exemption because he acknowledged that he would be willing to participate in an Islamic holy war.

Ali was stripped of his championship and prevented from fighting by every state athletic commission in the United States for three and a half years. In addition, he was criminally indicted and, on June 20, 1967, convicted of refusing induction into the U.S. armed forces and sentenced to five years in prison. Although he remained free on bail, four years passed before the U.S. Supreme Court overturned his conviction.

Meanwhile, as the 1960s grew more tumultuous, Ali's impact upon American society was growing, and he became a lightning rod for dissent. Ali's message of black pride and black resistance to white domination was on the cutting edge of the civil rights movement. Having refused induction into the U.S. Army, he also stood for the proposition that "unless you have a very good reason to kill, war is wrong." As black activist Julian Bond later observed, "When a figure as heroic and beloved as Muhammad Ali stood up and said, 'No, I won't go,' it reverberated through the whole society."

and openness. When Nixon's vice president, Spiro T. Agnew, was forced to resign from office in disgrace in 1973, the president appointed Ford to replace him. The Watergate scandal caused Nixon himself to resign on August 9, 1974, elevating Ford to the presidency. Ford thereby became the country's only chief executive who was not elected as either president or vice president. Less than a month later he granted Nixon a pardon for all crimes that he might have committed as president.

Another of Ford's early acts as president was the announcement of a conditional amnesty program for those who had evaded the draft or deserted during the Vietnam War. His program required up to two years of public service. When the program ended in 1975, only about one-fifth of those eligible had applied. Fewer than one-half of those granted amnesty had accepted its terms.

Congress denied Ford's request for aid to Indochina during the closing months of the Vietnam War. When South Vietnam fell to the North in April 1975, Ford ordered the evacuation of remaining American personnel. The simultaneous evacuation of thousands of Vietnamese orphans and refugees and their resettlement in the United States were widely criticized.

After leaving the White House in 1977, Ford retired from public life. He died on December 26, 2006, in Rancho Mirage, California.

CONCLUSION

Vietnam emerged from the war as a potent military power within Southeast Asia, but the costs of the conflict were enormous and long lasting. Its agriculture, business, and industry were disrupted, large parts of its countryside were scarred by bombs and defoliation and laced with land mines, and its cities and towns were heavily damaged.

On July 2, 1976, the country was officially united as the Socialist Republic of Vietnam. The communist government began to restructure the economy of the south. Large numbers of people fled the country. Hundreds of thousands more, mainly those who had been associated with the former government of South Vietnam or the Americans, were sent to jails or labor camps, and numerous others were forced to resettle in remote highland areas.

Vietnam was admitted to the United Nations in 1977. The country's main ally was the Soviet Union, and it sought to form close relationships with the communist governments of neighboring Laos and Cambodia. Cambodian resistance to Vietnamese demands led to full-scale warfare along the border, however, and Vietnam occupied the country in 1978. In response, China launched a brief invasion in 1979 across the Vietnamese border. Vietnam was almost entirely isolated from the international community. After the country withdrew its troops from Cambodia in 1989 and a peace settlement was achieved in 1991, Vietnam restored relations with Europe, China, Japan, and the countries of the Association of Southeast Asian Nations (ASEAN).

By 1992 Vietnam had altered its domestic and foreign policies significantly. Partly in response to the fall of communism in Eastern Europe and the Soviet Union, it had begun to modify its economic policies. The leaders of Vietnam sought foreign investment to help their economy. Diplomatic relations with the United States were formally restored in July 1995 after Vietnam agreed to pay compensation for confiscated U.S. property and the United States lifted a freeze on Vietnamese assets. That same month, Vietnam joined ASEAN. The country continued to liberalize its economy and enjoyed rapid economic growth and development. After more than a decade of negotiations, it became a member of the World Trade Organization in 2007.

GLOSSARY

abdicated Formally stepped down from the position of king or queen.

amnesty The granting of pardon (as by a government or president) to a large number of people.

autocracy Government in which one person has unlimited power.

bilateral Having or involving two sides or parties, such as a bilateral treaty.

bipartisan Representing, made up of, or organized by members of two political parties, as in a bipartisan foreign policy.

communism A system of government in which a single party controls state-owned means of production with the aim of establishing a stateless society. Also, a social system in which property and goods are owned in common.

coup A sudden and often violent overthrow of a government by a small group.

defoliation The stripping of leaves, especially prematurely.

dissident Disagreeing, especially with an established religious or political system, organization, or belief.

embargo Legal prohibition or restriction of trade.

emigrated Left a country or region to live elsewhere.

ethnic Of or relating to groups of people with common traits and customs and a sense of shared identity.

KEY FIGURES OF THE VIETNAM WAR

faction A group acting together within a larger body (such as a government).

guerrilla A member of a band of people engaged in warfare not as part of a regular army but as an independent unit making surprise raids behind enemy lines.

guillotine A machine for cutting off a person's head by means of a heavy blade sliding in two upright grooved posts.

insurgency Rebellion.

lycée French for "great school"; in France, it means an upper-level secondary school.

napalm A thickener used to make gasoline jellylike, as for use as bombs.

nationalistic Relating to or showing a belief that one's country is better and more important than other countries.

per capita By or for each person.

protectorate A small country or region that is ruled by a larger country.

ratified Gave legal or official approval to.

regime A form of government or administration; for instance, a totalitarian regime.

socialist A person, group, or country following any of various social systems based on shared or governmental ownership and administration of the means of production and distribution of goods.

GLOSSARY

strategic Of or relating to a general plan that is created to achieve a goal in war, politics, and so forth, usually over a long period of time.

tactical Relating to the science and art of setting up and maneuvering forces in combat.

venerate To show deep respect for.

vocational Of, relating to, or involved in training in a skill or trade to be followed as a career, as in a vocational school.

Watergate scandal After Richard Nixon won the U.S. presidential election in 1972, an investigation showed that he had been involved in illegal activities during the campaign. As a result of this scandal—known as Watergate—Nixon resigned from the presidency in 1974.

FOR MORE INFORMATION

National Archives and Records Administration

8601 Adelphi Road

College Park, MD 20740-6001

(866) 272-6272

Website: http://www.archives.gov

This federal agency stores historical documents, including photographs and correspondence, concerning American life and history. Its website on teaching with documents offers a glimpse of the Vietnam War through photographs (http://www.archives.gov/education/lessons/vietnam-photos).

National Museum of the United States Air Force

1100 Spaatz Street

Wright-Patterson AFB, OH 45433

(937) 255-3286

Website: http://www.nationalmuseum.af.mil

This organization is the official museum of the U.S. Air Force. Its website includes information about aircraft and weapons from the Vietnam War period at its Southeast Asia War page, http://www.nationalmuseum.af.mil/exhibits/sea/index.asp.

National Veterans Art Museum

4041 N. Milwaukee Avenue

FOR MORE INFORMATION

Chicago, IL 60641

(312) 326-0270

Website: http://www.nvam.org

This organization provides greater understanding of the impact of the Vietnam War on veterans by collecting, preserving, and exhibiting artwork that was created by veterans.

Veterans History Project

American Folklife Center of the Library of Congress

101 Independence Avenue SE

Washington, DC 20540-4615

(202) 707-4916

Website: http://www.loc.gov/vets

The Veterans History Project collects and preserves stories (personal narratives, correspondence, and visual memories) of wartime service, including that of the Vietnam War.

Vietnam Veterans Memorial Fund

2600 Virginia Avenue NW, Suite 104

Washington, DC 20037

(202) 393-0090

Website: http://www.vvmf.org

This commemorative website was created to extend the legacy of the Vietnam Veterans Memorial, which is located on the National Mall in Washington, D.C.

WEBSITES

Because of the changing nature of Internet links, Rosen Publishing has developed an online list of websites related to the subject of this book. This site is updated regularly. Please use this link to access the list:

http://www.rosenlinks.com/WAR/Viet

BIBLIOGRAPHY

Bond, Julian. *Vietnam: An Antiwar Comic Book.* Available online at www2.iath.virgina.edu/sixties/HTML_docs/Exhibits/Bond/Bond.html. 1967.

Caputo, Phil. *10,000 Days of Thunder: A History of the Vietnam War.* New York, NY: Atheneum, 2006.

George, Enzo. *The Vietnam Conflict: War with Communism.* New York, NY: Cavendish Square, 2014.

Gifford, Clive. *Why Did the Vietnam War Happen?* New York, NY: Gareth Stevens, 2011.

Gitlin, Marty. *U.S. Involvement in Vietnam.* Edina, MN: ABDO Publishing, 2010.

Hosch, William L. *The Korean War and the Vietnam War: People, Politics, and Power.* New York, NY: Britannica Educational Publishing, 2010.

Jeffrey, Gary. *The Vietnam War.* New York, NY: Crabtree Publishing Company, 2013.

Kent, Deborah. *The Vietnam War: From Da Nang to Saigon.* Berkeley Heights, NJ: Enslow, 2011.

Rau, Dana Meachen. *It's Cool to Learn About Countries: Vietnam.* Ann Arbor, MI: Cherry Lake Publishing, 2012.

Samuels, Charlie. *The Tet Offensive.* (Turning Points in U.S. Military History). New York, NY: Gareth Stevens, 2014.

INDEX

A

Agent Orange, 8, 45, 46
agriculture, 22–24
Ali, Muhammad, 50, 95–97
antiwar movement, 48–51, 52, 80–81
     key figures of, 92–97

B

boat people, 18

C

Calley, William, 42
Cambodia, 10, 28, 45, 53, 62, 64–66, 69–71, 88, 89, 99–100
China, 6, 10, 14, 15, 21, 27, 36, 40, 58, 59, 63, 99–100
Cold War, 8
communism/communists, 6–8, 21, 25, 26–27, 29, 31, 34, 44, 45, 51, 57, 58, 61, 62, 63, 64, 66, 67, 68, 69, 73–74, 84, 99–100

D

Diem, Ngo Dinh, 31, 32, 36, 57, 67–69, 72, 74, 75
doi moi, 21–22

F

Fonda, Jane, 94–95
Ford, Gerald, 88, 89-98
France, 6, 14, 15, 16, 28, 29–31, 58, 59, 61, 62, 63, 66, 72, 74

G

Giap, Vo Nguyen, 62–64
guerrillas/guerrilla warfare, 31, 32–36, 45, 59, 61, 71
Gulf of Tonkin Resolution, 38, 39, 79

H

Hanoi, 10, 20, 26, 31, 54, 56, 61, 63, 94
Ho Chi Minh, 29, 31, 32, 57–59, 62, 63, 68
Ho Chi Minh City (Saigon), 20, 26, 56, 74
Ho Chi Minh Trail, 40

I

Indochina wars, 31, 59, 63

J

Japan, 29, 58, 61
Johnson, Lyndon B., 38, 39–40, 52, 73, 78–82, 84, 85, 88

INDEX

K

Kennedy, John F., 36, 79
Khanh, Nguyen, 74–75
Khmer Rouge, 66–67, 69, 71
Kissinger, Henry, 52, 53, 61, 88–89, 88
Ky, Nguyen Cao, 36, 72, 75–77

L

Laos, 10, 28, 45, 53, 88, 99
Lon Nol, 69–71

M

McNamara, Robert S., 84–86
Minh, Duong Van, 74
My Lai Massacre, 42

N

Nixon, Richard M., 52, 54, 73, 82, 86–88, 89, 90, 98
North Vietnam
    bombing of by U.S., 40, 52, 53, 54, 79–80, 81–82, 85, 88
    communism and, 6, 21, 31
    division of Vietnam and, 31, 61, 63
    economy of, 21
    end of war and, 8, 53–57, 63–64, 74, 98
    key figures of, 57–67

P

Paris Peace Conferences, 61, 82, 88, 89
Pentagon Papers, 50

S

Saigon, 31, 51, 56, 58, 74, 84, 85
Sihanouk, Norodom, 64–67, 69, 71
South Vietnam
    division of Vietnam and, 31, 61
    economy of, 21
    end of war and, 53–56
    key figures of, 67–77

rule of Diem and guerrilla war in, 32–36, 68–69

surrender of/fall to North Korea, 56, 62, 64, 74, 77, 98

U.S. ground war in, 40

Soviet Union, 6, 8, 25, 36, 40, 53, 59, 99, 100

Spock, Benjamin, 92

T

Tet Offensive, 51–52, 84

Thieu, Nguyen Van, 36, 67, 72–74, 75, 77

Tho, Le Duc, 53, 59–62, 88, 89

U

United States

antiwar movement in, 48–51, 80–81

early involvement in Vietnam, 31, 36, 59, 61, 68, 69, 72, 75, 85

end of Vietnam War, 8, 53–54, 58, 64

enters war in Vietnam, 6, 8, 12, 14, 39–45, 58, 79

political and military leaders, 78–99

relationship with Vietnam after war, 25, 100

withdrawal of troops from Vietnam, 52–53, 54, 61, 73, 87, 89

V

Viet Cong, 8, 32–34, 39–40, 42, 44, 45, 51, 54, 59, 61, 69, 84, 85

Viet Minh, 29–31, 34, 58, 61, 63, 72

Vietnam

about, 10–28

as colony of France, 6, 28, 29–31, 58, 59, 61, 62, 63, 72, 74 division into North and South, 6, 21, 31, 57, 61, 63

economy of, 14, 20–26, 100

government of, 26–27

history of, 6, 27–28

land and climate of, 10–12

occupation of by Japan, 29, 58, 61

people and culture of, 14–20

plants and animals of, 12–14

reunification of after war, 8, 16, 21, 56, 62, 64, 99

Vietnam War

casualties of, 8–9, 48

cause of, 6–8

destruction caused by, 8, 12, 45, 46, 99

draft for, 50, 98

end of, 53–56, 58, 63–64, 73–74, 89, 90, 98

peace talks, 52, 53–54, 59, 61–62, 79–80, 81–82, 88, 89

U.S. entrance into, 39–45, 79

W

war of attrition, 44, 82

Westmoreland, William, 40, 41–44, 51, 82–84

World Trade Organization, 25, 100

5/20/16